Contents

About Horses   4

The Parts of a Horse   6

Colours   10

Learning to Ride   12

Looking After a Pony   18

Tack   20

How to Draw Horses   22

All Kinds of Horses   24

Ponies   26

Glossary   30

Index   32

If you find an unusual or difficult word in this book, check for an explanation in the glossary on pages 30 and 31.

About Horses

Did you know there are about 300 breeds of horses and ponies? They come in many different sizes, shapes and colours, as you will see here. But all of them can run or gallop quickly on their strong hooves, which are really just a special kind of middle toe. There are about 750 million horses in the world, not counting all the asses, donkeys, mules and zebras that also belong to the horse family!

A baby horse is called a foal until it is one year old, then it is known as a yearling. Its mother is a mare and its father is a stallion.

Stallion

Mare

Foal

KINGFISHER DIPPERS

Horses and Ponies

Stephen Attmore

Kingfisher Books

Kingfisher Books, Grisewood & Dempsey Ltd,
Elsley House, 24–30 Great Titchfield Street,
London W1P 7AD.

First published in 1989 by Kingfisher Books

BRITISH LIBRARY CATALOGUING IN PUBLICATION DATA
Attmore, Stephen
  Horses and ponies.
  1. Horses – For children   2. Livestock:
  Ponies – For children
  I. Title
  599.72′5
ISBN 0-86272-378-7

Series editor: Jacqui Bailey
Designed by Ben White
Cover design by David Jefferis
Text edited by Meg Sanders
Illustrated by Elizabeth Turner/*Thornton Artists;*
    Sheila Ratcliffe/*Maggie Mundy Agency;*
    Drawing Attention; Peter Stephenson/*Jillian Burgess*

Phototypeset by Southern Positives and Negatives (SPAN),
Lingfield, Surrey
Printed in Spain

Icelandic
pony

Shetland
pony

Ponies are small horses that
are no higher than 14.2 hands
(see below). A Shetland pony is
only about nine hands high. As
most ponies are gentle and
sensible they are good animals
for children to learn to ride.

*A measuring stick is used
to measure a horse or
pony from the ground to
the top of its withers (see
the diagram on the next
page). The height is given
in 'hands'. A hand is equal
to 10 centimetres. Try
measuring a pony using
your hands as shown in
the circle.*

The Parts of a Horse

The different parts of a horse are called points. All types and breeds have the same points, all with special names (see below). Together, the points of a horse make up its conformation – the way it looks. A horse can have a good or bad conformation. A horse with a bad conformation may have knock knees, a hollow back, a thick neck or an extra large head. A horse of good conformation looks good because its parts are of the right size and shape.

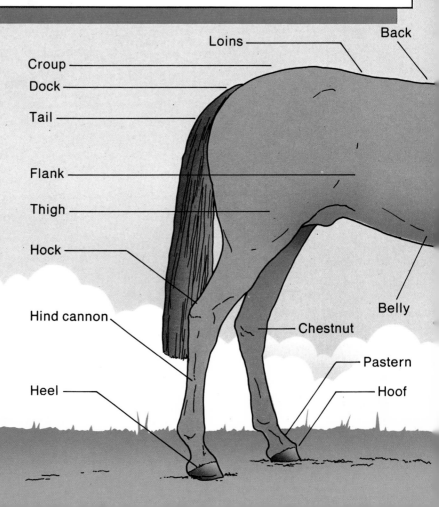

Loins

Back

Croup

Dock

Tail

Flank

Thigh

Hock

Belly

Hind cannon

Chestnut

Pastern

Heel

Hoof

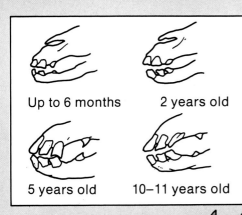

Up to 6 months   **2 years old**

5 years old   **10–11 years old**

HOW OLD IS A HORSE?

You can tell the age of a horse or pony by looking at its teeth. Small baby teeth come through soon after it is born. By the age of five a horse has a full set of big adult teeth. As it gets older the teeth grow longer.

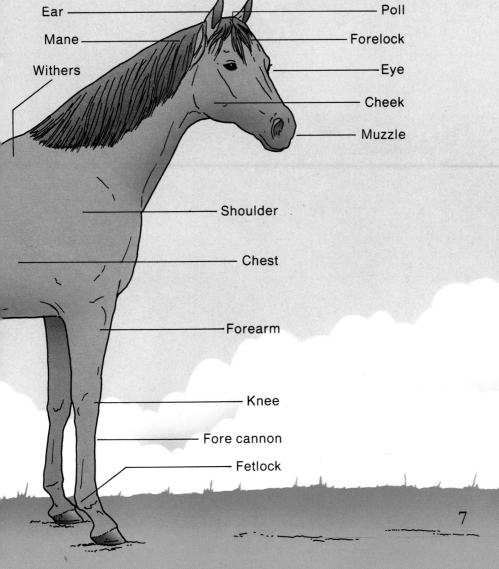

Ear — Poll

Mane — Forelock

Withers — Eye

Cheek

Muzzle

Shoulder

Chest

Forearm

Knee

Fore cannon

Fetlock

The Parts of a Horse – 2

When you look at horses and ponies you will see that many of them have markings on their heads, bodies and legs. A horse that is just one colour with no other markings is said to be 'whole-coloured'.

Some horses have hairless, pink patches on their muzzles or lips. These are known as 'flesh-marks'. White patches on the horse's head or legs often have special names – some of them are shown here. But a white patch anywhere else on the horse's body is simply known as a 'white patch'.

LEG MARKINGS
A white marking that goes right up the leg is called a 'full stocking'. If it reaches up to the knee or hock it is just a stocking.

1. Stocking
2. Fetlock
3. Coronet
4. Pastern
5. Heel
6. Sock

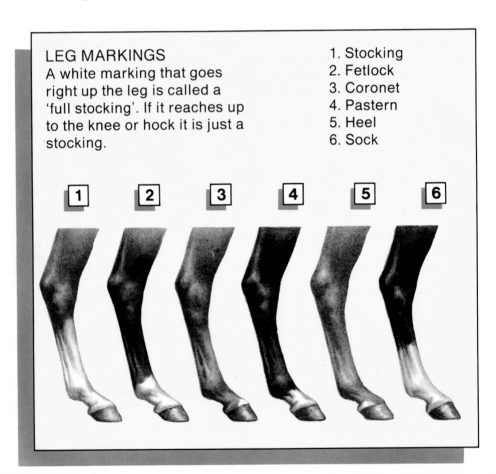

Star

Stripe

Blaze

Snip

White
face

The names of head markings often give a clue to their
shape, but a mark on the forehead of a horse or pony is
called a 'star', even if it is not exactly star-shaped. A
'stripe' is the name given to a white line running down
the centre of the face.

A wide band of white running down the face is called a
'blaze'. If the white spreads out around the eyes and to
the sides of the face, it is known as a 'white face', while a
'snip' is a small white mark on the muzzle.

Colours

Strawberry roan

Chestnut

Chestnuts are red-brown.
The colour can vary from dark
brown to gold. They never have
black legs, mane or tail.

Roans have white hairs
mixed with another colour in
their coats. The three shades
are strawberry, bay and blue.

Piebald

Skewbald

Cream

A piebald horse or pony has
large black and white patches.
A skewbald is brown and white
or brown, black and white.

Cream is an unusual colour.
Horses and ponies this colour
have creamy coats, manes and
tails and pink eyes.

Brown

Dun

Palomino

Brown horses also have brown manes, tails and legs. Duns are often sandy-coloured with black manes and tails.

The Palomino has a beautiful golden coat with a silvery mane and tail. The foals tend to darken in colour with age.

Black

Grey

Bay

A bay horse is brown with a black mane and tail. Its legs are also black, usually from the knees and hocks down.

A black horse is black all over. A grey horse has black and white hairs mixed in its coat. It must have one grey parent.

Learning to Ride

Leaping onto a horse and galloping off like the cowboys do is very exciting, but unless you want to land on the ground again the hard way, it is a good idea to learn how to ride properly first.

If possible, go to a good riding school and have as many lessons as you can. Visit the school with your parents before booking any lessons, and watch a class in action. Then you will know what to expect when you have your first lesson.

◄ After several lessons you may be able to go riding around the local countryside. This sort of riding is called hacking. On roads, stay in single file to keep out of the way of cars.

► A good way to start riding is with the instructor leading the pony on a long rein. This means you won't have to worry about where it is going while you are learning to stay in the saddle. You may feel nervous at first but don't be afraid to say so – the instructor will understand.

Learning to Ride – 2

▲ Wrong. You should not wear clothes like these for riding.

▲ Right. The correct type of clothes to wear for riding.

You will not be expected to have a complete riding outfit when you go for your first lesson. But you will need a riding hat or skull cap. Although riding schools often hire them out, it is best to have your own as it must fit your head properly. Your jacket should be loose enough to let you move around, but not so large as to flap about and frighten your pony.

Corduroy or woollen trousers are more comfortable than jeans, which may rub the inside of your knees when you grip the saddle. You will find it easier to mount your pony (see below) if your trousers are not too tight. Do not wear high-heeled or slip-on shoes. Lace-up walking shoes are best. If they have a small heel your feet are less likely to slip out of the stirrups. Best of all are jodhpur boots, and it is worth buying a pair if you can. Gloves are a good idea for outdoor riding.

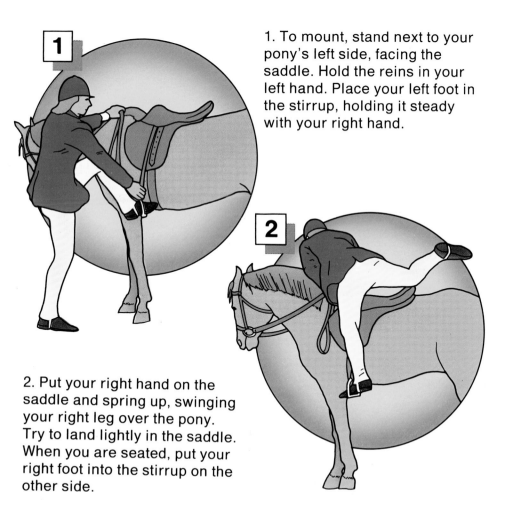

1. To mount, stand next to your pony's left side, facing the saddle. Hold the reins in your left hand. Place your left foot in the stirrup, holding it steady with your right hand.

2. Put your right hand on the saddle and spring up, swinging your right leg over the pony. Try to land lightly in the saddle. When you are seated, put your right foot into the stirrup on the other side.

Walk

Trot

HOLDING THE REINS

This is the correct way to hold the reins. You can practise at home with two chairs. Tie some string reins to one chair and sit astride the other.

Learning to Ride – 3

When you are on your pony, it is important that you sit in the correct position in the saddle. Here are some things to remember that might help you. First, you must sit in the deepest part of the saddle. Hold your head up and your shoulders back. Keep the inside of your thighs against the saddle but do not grip too tightly. Try not to lean forward. Second, hold the reins down, close to the pony's withers.

Look at the rider shown in the picture at the top left of this page. You could draw a straight line from the rider's shoulders, down the back, through the seat to the heels. This is the correct position.

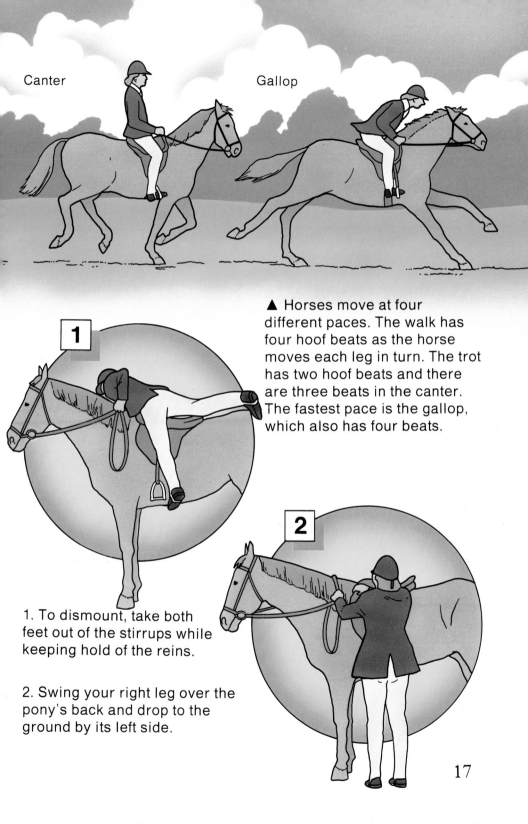

Canter

Gallop

1

2

▲ Horses move at four different paces. The walk has four hoof beats as the horse moves each leg in turn. The trot has two hoof beats and there are three beats in the canter. The fastest pace is the gallop, which also has four beats.

1. To dismount, take both feet out of the stirrups while keeping hold of the reins.

2. Swing your right leg over the pony's back and drop to the ground by its left side.

17

Looking After a Pony

Looking after a pony is hard work. A pony kept in a stable needs fresh water, food and exercise each day. Cleaning the stable, or mucking out, is a daily task too. A pony kept in a field also needs some shelter and a good supply of fresh water. Check each day to make sure it has not hurt itself, and that the paddock gate and fences are in good repair.

Grooming tones up your pony's muscles as well as keeping its coat clean. For both horse and rider, grooming is a good time to get to know each other.

A pony kept in a loose box needs plenty of hay and regular feeds of corn and bran. The box or stable must be cleared of dirty straw every morning, and fresh straw put in its place.

The dandy brush, body brush, comb, water brush and stable rubber are used for grooming. The hoofs are cleaned with a metal pick. The curry comb is for cleaning the brushes.

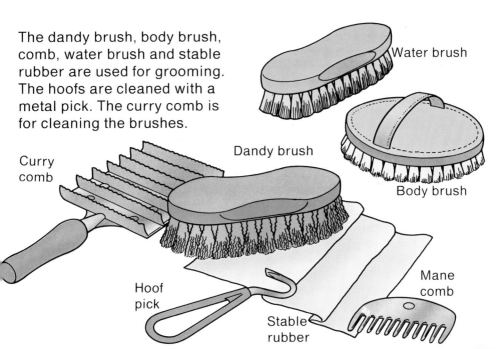

Water brush

Dandy brush

Body brush

Curry comb

Hoof pick

Stable rubber

Mane comb

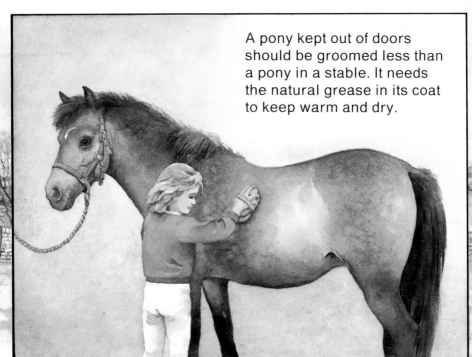

A pony kept out of doors should be groomed less than a pony in a stable. It needs the natural grease in its coat to keep warm and dry.

19

Tack

Tack is the name for saddles, bridles and other things needed for riding. The saddle is important because it spreads your weight evenly over the pony's back. The bridle and reins are used to control the pony and to tell it what you want it to do.

Before you start off, the tack is adjusted with straps and buckles to make you and your pony feel comfortable. You will soon get used to the feel of the tack, and be able to adjust it yourself.

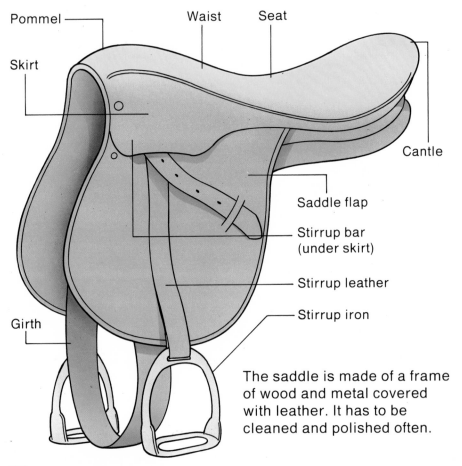

Pommel

Skirt

Waist

Seat

Cantle

Saddle flap

Stirrup bar
(under skirt)

Stirrup leather

Stirrup iron

Girth

The saddle is made of a frame of wood and metal covered with leather. It has to be cleaned and polished often.

The bridle is the leather headpiece that slips over the horse's head and the reins are attached to it. The bit is a rubber or metal bar which fits inside the horse's mouth.

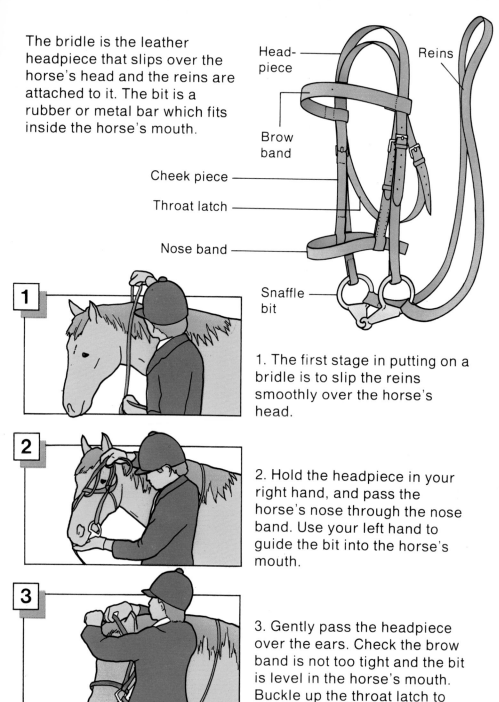

Head-piece

Reins

Brow band

Cheek piece

Throat latch

Nose band

Snaffle bit

1

1. The first stage in putting on a bridle is to slip the reins smoothly over the horse's head.

2

2. Hold the headpiece in your right hand, and pass the horse's nose through the nose band. Use your left hand to guide the bit into the horse's mouth.

3

3. Gently pass the headpiece over the ears. Check the brow band is not too tight and the bit is level in the horse's mouth. Buckle up the throat latch to hold it all in place.

21

How to Draw Horses

It is great fun to draw horses, and not difficult –
when you know how. Follow the stages shown here
and start with simple shapes. Draw three ovals, one
smaller than the others, and join them with curved
lines to form the body and head. Then you can put in
the details. Follow the diagrams on the opposite page
to draw a head in close-up.

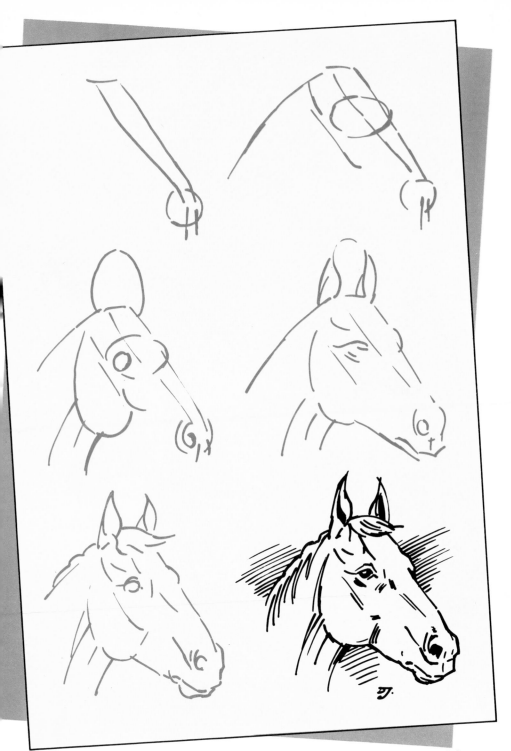

All Kinds of Horses

There are hundreds of different horses, divided into types and breeds. The type depends on how it is used. The breeds range from the tiny Falabella (under seven hands) to the Shire horse (over 17 hands). Here are just a few breeds from around the world.

Draught horses are the world's strongest animals, except for elephants. The Percheron is a hard-working French breed. The English Shire horse is the tallest breed in the world. Some are 19 hands high.

Percheron

Shire

Friesian

THE ROCKING HORSE
Did you know that the mighty Percheron was used as a model for the first rocking horses ever made? Luckily they weren't made to life size.
It is also a little known fact that horses can go to sleep standing up. They don't need any rocking!

The Friesian is bred in the Netherlands. Long ago it was ridden into battle by knights.

Thoroughbred   Arab   Morgan

Thoroughbreds were first bred in England for racing. All the Thoroughbreds in the world were originally bred from three Arab stallions.

Arabs are one of the oldest and most beautiful breeds in the world. The Morgan is a sturdy American horse. It is a popular family horse.

American Saddlebred

Lipizzaner

Camargue   Lusitano

Camargue horses live in almost wild herds in southern France. The American Saddle-bred is a show-ring horse with a high-stepping gait (walk).

The Lusitano from Portugal is known for its bravery in the bull ring. Lipizzaners learn clever tricks at the Spanish Riding School in Vienna.

Ponies

Strong, sturdy ponies are used as working animals in many countries. Haflinger ponies, for example, pull heavy loads up the snowy mountains of Austria. Some ponies are very small indeed. The Falabella (see page 28) is the world's tiniest horse, yet it can outrun a racehorse over a short distance.

Criollo

Haflinger

The Criollo is ridden by cowboys in South America. It originally came from Spain.

The Haflinger is 14 hands high. It may live to a great age and can be chestnut or Palomino.

Fjording

Welsh Cob

Shetland

The Fjording is a Norwegian dun pony with a black stripe down its back.

Welsh Cobs are strong, active ponies, used for farm work or pulling carriages.

The Shetland is one of the smallest breeds – only nine hands high.

Sumba (Indonesia)

Hocaido (Japan)

Pinto (North and South America)

Pony of the Americas

The Pinto (or Painted Horse) was bred by American Indians as a war horse. It is either piebald or skewbald.

This tiny pony is under seven hands high. The Falabella was first bred in Argentina about 40 years ago as a family pet.

SOMETHING TO DO
Make your own book about horses and ponies or start a scrapbook. You could copy pictures from this book or collect magazine pictures. Write down all the things you can find out about each type of horse.

Ponies – 2

The Pony of the Americas was bred quite recently to be a small child's pony.

The Hocaido is a Japanese pony known for its speed. Sumba ponies are used not only for working but also for dancing. Bells are put around their ankles and, usually with a child upon their back, they will dance to the sound of tom-tom drums.

Glossary

Bay
A coat colour. The body is chestnut brown while the lower legs, mane and tail are black.

Bit
Metal or rubber part of the bridle which fits into the horse's mouth. It gives the rider control over the horse's pace and direction.

Breeds
Groups of horses or ponies that have been bred to have a particular shape, colour or characteristic.

Bridle
Part of the tack placed over the horse's head. Attached to it are the reins and the bit. There are several types of bridle.

Cantle
The back of the saddle.

Chestnut
A coat colour, or a small point on the inside of a horse's leg.

Cob
A horse or pony with good conformation: a compact body with a strong back and short legs.

Colt
A male horse under four years of age.

Conformation
The shape of a horse's body.

Coronet
The point at which the hoof joins the foot.

Dun
A coat colour with yellow in it. The legs, mane and tail are often black.

Filly
A female horse under four years of age.

Foal
A horse or pony up to one year old.

Gaits
The paces a horse moves at (walk, trot, canter, gallop).

Girth
A band made of leather, webbing or nylon fixed to the saddle. It passes under the belly and keeps the saddle in position.

Hand
The unit by which horses are measured. It is about 10 centimetres (the width of an adult's hand).

Hock
The joint at the top of the cannon bone on the hind leg.

Mare
Female horse or pony over four years old.

Muzzle
Part of the horse's head including the nose and mouth.

Pastern
Part of the horse's leg between the fetlock and the hoof. It is made up of lots of small bones.

Points
The parts of a horse's body. They are always the same for every horse.

Pommel
The front part of the saddle which sticks up.

Pony
Male or female horse not over 14.2 hands high.

Reins
These are held by the rider and are connected to the bridle. They help the rider to guide the horse.

Stallion
Male horse over four years of age, used for breeding.

Stirrup
The leather strap on either side of a saddle which holds the stirrup iron in place. A rider puts his or her feet in the stirrup irons.

Tack
Saddles, bridles etc. It is short for tackle.

Tree
The wooden frame on which a saddle is built.

Withers
The ridge between the shoulders of a horse.

Index

age of a pony   7
Arab horses   25

bay   11, 30
bit   21, 30
bridle   20, 21, 30

Camargue   25
cantle   20, 30
chestnut   6, 10, 30
cob   30
colours   10–11
colt   30
conformation   6, 30
coronet   6
Criollo   26

draught horses   24, 31
dun   11, 30

Falabella   24, 26, 28
filly   30
Fjording pony   27
foal   4, 30
Friesian   24

girth   20, 31
grooming   18, 19

Haflinger pony   26
head markings   9
Hocaido   28
hock   6, 31
hooves   4, 6, 19

Icelandic pony   5

leg markings   8
Lipizzaner   25
Lusitano   25

mare   4, 31
measuring a pony   5
Morgan   25
mounting/dismounting   15, 17

Palomino   11, 26
Percheron   24
Pinto   28
points of a horse   6, 31
Pony of the Americas   28

reins   15, 16, 17, 31
riding clothes   14–15
riding lessons   12–13

Saddlebred, American   25
saddles   15–17, 20
Shetland pony   5, 27
Shire   24
skull cap   14
stables   18–19
stallion   4, 31
stirrups   15, 17, 21, 22, 31
Sumba   28

Thoroughbreds   25
tree   20, 31

Welsh Cob pony   27
withers   6, 31